How to Make the Best Butter

MODERN DAIRYMEN

—USE—

HIGGIN'S EUREKA FINE SALT.

ENGLISH

HIGH GRADE,

THE STANDARD SALT FOR DAIRY AND HOUSEHOLD PURPOSES.

GOLD MEDALS AND HIGHEST AWARDS
At the great Fairs of the World.

Philadelphia, 1876.

LONDON, 1879.

MELBOURNE, 1881.

LONDON, 1882.

New Zealand, 1882.

PARIS, 1878.

DUBLIN, 1879.

ADELAIDE, 1881.

LONDON, 1882.

LONDON, 1884.

NEW ORLEANS, 1885.

Butter and Cheese salted with it carried the highest premiums over anything else wherever put in competition.

These awards were made by juries composed of practical, scientific and conscientious men.

HOW TO MAKE THE BEST BUTTER.

Good butter may be made under quite unfavorable conditions; better butter may be made under better conditions; but the best butter is made under only the best conditions, and by the most skillful manipulation.

THE HERD.

I shall not give the preference to any breed. It is only necessary that cream should be rich in fat, and churn easily. These qualities may be possessed by the cream of the milk from any of the breeds Even elephant's milk is said to be superior in this respect. These qualities can be practically ascertained only by the test of the churn. Of course, the cream must be rich in flavor, and free from the bitter taste peculiar to the cream and milk of some cows.

THE FEED

As milk is made from the food which the cow eats, and partakes more or less of the quality and flavor of the food, it follows that cows must run in clean, sweet pastures in summer, and that the cows get hold of no rank flavored vegetation, either in the pasture or on the road to the barn-yard or stable where the milking is done. Just the nipping of mal-flavored herbage on the way to and from the pasture has been known to give a bad flavor to the milk, and to the products manufactured from it Even the breathing of air passing over carrion, or an onion field has been found to taint the milk of the cows thus inhaling it. Salt should be regularly given to

3

the cows A better way is to put the salt where the cows can go and lick it at any time. They will not take too much when it is always present But when it is given to them occasionally, they will eat to excess, and thus induce thirst and fever, that interfere with the operation of milk secretion The stronger cows will thrust aside the weaker ones, so that the latter will not get salt enough, while the former are gorging with it For this reason if salt is not kept regularly within the reach of the cows the better way is to salt them in the stalls, where each gets just what is given to her, and no more Salt is not only essential to the health of the cow, aiding digestion and assimilation, but affects the churning of the cream A lack of salt for the cows will make hard churning, and trouble in this way might often be obviated by giving the cows a proper amount of salt

Iu winter special care should be taken to give the cows the right kinds of food, in the right proportions, so that the nitrogenous, or milk and muscle producing foods shall bear a proper relation to the amount of carbonaceous, or heat and fat-producing foods Early-cut hay—say timothy or orchard grass, with a mixture of clover and other sweet grasses—if supplemented with corn meal and oatmeal, or corn meal and wheat bran, mixed in equal proportions by weight, will make a good feed for butter. It is well, however, to always have a little sweet ensilage, or beets, or other succulent food, and give the cows a mess of it once a day. It will, as a relish, not only aid digestion and promote health—and whatever promotes health aids in milk secretion—but improves the churning quality of the cream , for it has been found that all dry feed makes hard churning, and causes a waste of the fats in the buttermilk, and this can be prevented by giving the cows juicy, succulent food with their dry hay and grain.

THE DRINK

It is important that the cow should have plenty of clean water to drink, and that she should not be put to too much trouble to get it If she is she will often get very thirsty before she drinks, and then will drink so much as to make her feverish and uncomfortable—a condition not favorable to milk secretion. Do not let your cows drink out of stagnant ponds or pools. If you do the spores of algæ, which are microscopic, will enter into the circulation of the cow, and appear in her milk, rendering it unwholesome for human food, and of course injuring its products. In winter it will be found of advantage to take the chill off from the water given to the cow, and to prevent her getting chilled when she goes to drink Chilling the cow shrinks the flow of milk and reduces its quality. It takes an extra amount of feed to raise the temperature of the animal organism after it has been reduced by chilling. It therefore pays to keep the cows as comfortable and contented as possible.

SURROUNDINGS.

All the surroundings must be kept clean and sweet. The droppings must be promptly cleared away, and absorbents—such as dry earth, sawdust, land plaster, dry muck, etc —must be freely used in the stable or milking shed No animal or vegetable matter must be allowed to decay in the vicinity of where the cows are milked, nor where they can breathe the atmosphere that is loaded with the bacteria rising from the decaying matter. Nor must the milk be allowed to stand in such an atmosphere, so these bacteria can drop into it, and there begin the work of decomposition, by feeding on the nitrogenous portions of the milk

VENTILATION

Too much attention cannot be paid to keeping the cows supplied with pure, sweet air The supply of air should come in at the cows' heads and pass off at the rear But most stables are arranged to let the air in at the rear of the cows, where, being heavier than the warm air inside, it drops down and takes up the vapor and odors of the droppings, along with the exhalations from the cows' bodies, and bears them along to their heads, to be drawn into their lungs and mingled with their blood at every breath Fifteen minutes of such inhalation, Prof. L B Arnold declares, will taint the milk immediately thereafter drawn from the cows' udders, and give it "a taste of the barn-yard." People who are otherwise cleanly are often troubled with this taste in their milk, which they cannot account for, when all the trouble lies in the bad ventilation, or no ventilation, of their stables, or of whatever place they milk in. There should be a free circulation of air, avoiding drafts, and a place for the escape of all foul odors as fast as they rise, without their being permitted to load the air which the cows breathe. Better apply a little artificial heat than keep your cows cooped up in a smothering atmosphere, which is inimical both to the health of the animal and the production of the best of milk. Sweet food, sweet water, and sweet air, are absolutely essential to the production of the best butter.

CLEANLINESS

As might be inferred from what has gone before, absolute cleanliness is indispensable. Most people have some idea of cleanliness, but not the same ideas. The term is comparative and admits of degrees of application. But while all have some ideas of cleanliness,

I have sometimes thought that some people have no idea of nastiness To them as is said to be the case with the pure in heart, all things are pure, I will, therefore, try to give you some idea of what I mean by cleanliness To begin with, the person should be clean enough not to emit offensive odors. The clothing should have like freedom from bad odors, and have no dirt adhering to it that may rattle off and drop into the milk. All loose dirt and hairs should be brushed from the side, flank and udder of the cow, that it may not drop into the milk If there is filth on the cow's udder that cannot be brushed or wiped off, it should be washed off, not with milk drawn from the teat, but with water near by in another pail than the one to be milked in. As I like to have the hairs and the butter kept apart on the table, so I like to have the filth and milk kept apart in the stable. Proceed to milk gently, quietly, and briskly, avoiding everything liable to hurt or irritate the cow. In no case depend on the strainer to take out dirt, for some of it will dissolve, if it gets into the milk, and cannot be strained out Only loose particles held mechanically, can be taken out by the strainer. The rest will remain to injure the flavor of the product. Therefore keep the dirt out, and strain the milk to take out such floating hairs or particles as your vigilance fails to keep out Rinse all things—strainers, pails, cans, churns, cream pots, skimmers, and so on—with cold water as soon as used. Then give them a thorough washing before they dry, in water as warm as the hands can bear, and put a little sal soda, ammonia, or other alkali, in the water, to cut the grease on the articles washed. After this washing scald them in boiling water and set them out in the pure air—in the sunshine if possible—to dry and aerate If they are wiped, let the wiping be done with a perfectly clean cloth, not before used since being thoroughly washed and boiled. Set the holloware on its side, the open end turned a little downward, so that floating spores and particles of dirt will not settle down in them and find a resting place

If anything were necessary to enforce the importance of cleanliness and a pure atmosphere in connection with milk at all stages, perhaps it will be found in the fact that lack of cleanliness leads to early decay of milk or of its products, and this decay in some, if not in all cases, developes the poison which makes cheese and other decaying animal products poisonous. Until recently, it has not been known what the element is that makes cheese, sausage, salt fish, etc., poisonous But by investigations made by Dr Victor C Vaughan, Professor of Chemistry in the Michigan University, he has discovered the crystals of a very powerful poison in poisonous cheese, and he calls this poison *tyrotoxicon*. He has also found the same element in poisonous ice cream, both the product of decomposing milk, or of the constituents of milk. He traces this class of

6

decay to ferments introduced through lack of cleanliness, and urges upon dairymen the greatest care in this direction No doubt the use of pure salt, instead of the cheap stuff which so many dairymen consider good enough, would go far toward preventing the development of the powerful poison now called *tyroticon*. A hint to the wise ought to be sufficient.

HANDLING THE MILK

The sooner after the milk is drawn from the cow it is strained and set for cream-raising the better. The less agitation and the less reduction of temperature, the more rapid and complete will be the separation of cream Carrying milk long distances is a disadvantage , and if the temperature is much run down, it should be raised again before setting, or immediately after, by artificial means This gives a wide range for the temperature to fall, and cream always rises best in a falling temperature. It rises very slowly if the temperature is stationary, and little or not at all if the temperature is rising. It is well to bear these facts in mind and avoid the unfavorable conditions.

MODE OF SETTING.

If I aimed to make the best butter regardless of the quantity, I should set my milk shallow, and in cold air. This does not secure the greatest yield, I am told, but it does secure the best flavor, for the reason that it affords the best conditions for the aeration and ripening of the cream by oxidation. Such cream will make good, sweet cream butter, with good keeping qualities But where cream is raised by submerging, or even deep setting without submerging, it must be soured to develop flavor, otherwise it will have only a cream flavor, delicate and evanescent, instead of the rich flavor imparted by oxidation. But in deep setting without submerging, or shallow setting in water, the air in the room must be kept very pure and sweet, or bad odors and bacteria will be taken up by the cream, While the milk remains warmer than the air, it gives off vapor which the air takes up, and the milk is thus purified ; but as soon as the milk gets colder than the air in the room, a reverse action takes place, the vapors in the air are condensed on the surface of the milk, which absorbs whatever odors or impurities there are in it, and thus the air is purified instead of the milk, which is constantly deteriorating

CENTRIFUGE,

There is another way of getting the cream out of the milk, and that is by the use of the centrifugal machine. This is perhaps too expensive a method for the small dairyman, but is understood to work well in large dairies and factories. There is some dispute about the effect of the machine on the quality of the product ; but I suspect much that has been attributed to the machine is owing to other causes, depending on the skill and judgment of the operator. It is understood that cream obtained by the separator has to be soured and ripened before churning

WHEN TO SKIM

I should always skim the cream off from the milk before souring, certainly before coagulation. Most butter makers, I believe, prefer skimming just as the milk begins to sour I would prefer to have it done just before the milk begins to sour, and then get the cream just as free from milk or caseous matter as possible. Two elements in milk militate against keeping sweet the butter made from it These are albumen and sugar—both unstable elements If we can keep these out or get them out, there is no reason why the butter should not keep for a long time By skimming the milk while it is yet sweet and perfectly fluid, we shall be able to get the cream with a minimum amount of milk in it, and therefore with a minimum amount of sugar and albumen in it, as well as of caseous matter. This I consider an important point, and hence I would skim the milk before any acidity appears If the cream is too stiff to churn, dilute it with warm water

PREPARING CREAM.

If cream is to be kept any length of time it should be reduced to a temperature below 55 degrees Fahrenheit At 50 degrees the change would be so slow that the cream might be kept for several days But every addition of cream should be accompanied with a thorough stirring of the whole mass, to mix evenly the old and new cream. Before churning the cream should be set where it will attain and retain a temperature of 60 degrees, or a little above ; but no additions of any cream should be made after the temperature is raised I have no doubt that trouble in churning sometimes arises from the fat globules not being as warm as the serum on which they float. Fat is a poor and therefore slow conductor or absorbent of heat. Where cream has been kept at a low temperature and is raised to the churning-point in a short time, I suspect that the fat globules sometimes fail to get warmed up to that point Hence unle s the cream stands at 60 degrees or above for considerable time, I would recommend raising the temperature of the cream a few degrees above the churning point In this way the desired temperature of the fat globules would be secured, and I think slow and vexatious churning often obviated Frequent stirrings will help equalize the temperature and secure an even souring or ripening of

8

the whole mass. At the first signs of acidity, I should commence the churning, at such temperature as the season of the year and my every-day experience indicated as the right one. I should use the kind of churn which I found most convenient and best. We do not yet quite know whether it is friction or concussion which causes the butter to come. But a good churn will agitate every particle of cream put into it, leaving none adhering to corners or ends to be wasted in the buttermilk.

CHARACTER OF BUTTER FAT.

It has long been a subject of discussion as to whether the butter globule has a caseous or membraneous covering or not. Experiments made by Dr. Babcock, of the New York Experiment Station, during the past season seem to settle this question. He finds they are liquid drops of fat held in the milk, without any covering at all save what the milk affords. As the albumen is the most viscous substance in the milk, it is not unlikely that this adheres to the drops of fat, giving them the appearance of having an envelope. He found that by raising the temperature and agitating the milk, he could divide these microscopic drops, making Jersey fat globules as fine as those of Holstein-Friesian or Ayershire milk, and even finer ; and by lowering the temprature to the right degree, the globules would unite, becoming double and treble their natural size—and, indeed, continuing to double up until they were visible to the eye, and appeared as butter.

Further, Dr. Babcock was able to make emulsions of different fats, and make them appear in the same way. Churning them at too high a temperature further divided the drops, and at a lower temperature united them into the consistency of butter. But emulsions of different kinds of fats required different temperatures for churning. Too high a temperature would further divide the globules, and too low a temperature would prevent their cohesion at all.

CHURNING.

We have here some hints about churning. The temperature must be right—neither too high nor too low. If too high, we would beat the globules into smaller ones ; if too low they would refuse to unite ; and in either case the butter would fail to appear. Milk in different conditions and at different seasons of the year would call for a different temperature within a moderate range. If the cream is viscous and ropy, as it sometimes is when the cold weather comes, or when the systems of the cows receive any sudden shock, from chilling, a higher temperature would be called for and a dilution of the cream with warm water would help dissolve and wash off the albuminous matter adhering to the fat globules,

9

thus letting them free to come together and coalesce. This seems to be the philosophy of churning, viewed in the light of recent experiments, and it suggests the idea that there may be an advantage, where the temperature of cream has been run down low, to raise the temperature a few degrees above the churning point, as before suggested, and then let it settle down to the right degree before beginning to churn. If this is not done, the fat, being a poorer conductor of heat than the serum in which it floats, may be still in a solid instead of a semi-solid condition—and the point just between a congealing and a liquid state I take to be the right one for churning

WASHING AND SALTING BUTTER.

It is not many years since that dairymen thought it necessary to gather their butter into a solid mass in the churn, and then take it out and work and wash it as long as the water looked milky. A few years ago some one started the idea of stopping the churn when the butter gathered into lumps the size of beechnuts or kernels of corn. In this condition it was washed in the churn or bowl, with but little working until the salt was applied This was an improvement. But now the more advanced butter makers stop the churn as soon as the butter appears in granules of the size of wheat kernels, and even as small as mustard seed.

A very successful butter maker says he was not able to get the butter to take the salt properly, or as evenly as he wanted it to do, if he allowed the granules to become larger than mustard seed If larger than this, a magnifying glass would show white spots of unsalted butter. His practice is—and it is the practice of most good butter makers—to draw off the buttermilk immediately on stopping the churn, and then pour into the churn enough water, at 55 degrees or below, to float the butter, when the churn is greatly agitated a few moments, and the water drawn off The second washing, done in the same way, is with brine, made of the purest salt that can be obtained 1½ lbs of salt to two gallons of water will make about the proper strength of brine for this purpose.

When butter is treated in the way described, no working at all is required. It is only necessary to repeat the washings until the water runs clear   Nothing like gathering or packing the butter should be done If the water is cold enough, there will be no adhesion of the granules. They will remain distinct, and can be stirred around in the water floating them with perfect ease ; and when the water is well drawn off, they can be ladled out of the churn and placed on the table or butter-worker without packing them in the least. In this condition they are prepared to receive the salt ; but the butter should be allowed to stand, either in the churn or on the table, until the water is all drained out that will In half an hour or an hour the butter, piled in a mass, will drain sufficiently dry. It is not desirable to get all the water out Enough should be left in the butter to dissolve the salt and make sufficient brine to penetrate the whole mass. But if more water than is necessary is left in the butter, unless an extra amount of salt is used, the brine made by the dissolving the salt will be a weak one, and no matter how much or how little may be worked out, what remains will be weak and therefore imperfectly salt the butter. Care should be taken that the amount of water in the butter and the amount of salt used are so proportioned that a saturated brine will be produced. More salt than this will make the butter gritty with undissolved salt.

Many suppose that when it comes to salting the butter, it should be pressed into a compact form, spread out in a thin sheet, and have the salt sprinkled over it. Then have this sheet rolled up into a cylinder, which is then flattened out into a thin sheet again, more salt sprinkled on, and again rolled into a solid cylinder. After the salt is rolled in, by this process, the level is brought to bear and the butter worked until the salt is supposed to be evenly incorporated Then many set the butter aside, for twelve or twenty-four hours, when it is brought out and again worked, to get out any white streaks that may appear.

Now, this may be a good way, if the salt is to be " worked in." But there is a more excellent method It is to *stir* the salt into the the butter, while the latter is still in the granular form. Most of the leading dairymen are omitting the "second working," and packing their butter directly into the tub, thus saving labor, avoiding injury to what is called the "grain" of the butter, and saving salt by retaining in the butter all that is put in With either a first or second working, it is possible to work out a large amount of brine, thus leaving the butter too fresh, unless an extra amount of salt is put in.

To avoid this waste, some dairymen, supposing the salt must be "worked in," have resorted to coarse-grained salt, after the manner of cheese makers who salt their curd before the surplus whey is drained out In this the butter makers make a great mistake, in two particulars. First, in working their butter with undissolved salt in it, they do great injury to the texture, which is also an injury to the flavor and to the keeping quality of the butter So far as the texture is concerned, they might as well work in so much sand. The undissolved salt scours the butter and cuts the "grain," giving the butter a greasy, shiny appearance which is as offensive to the experienced eye as the loss of flavor is to the educated palate

The second point of injury arising from using coarse salt is the leaving of undissolved salt in the butter to make it gritty. The

11

harder the salt the worse. Unless a good deal of water is left in the butter and the butter is allowed to stand a good while and is worked a good deal, to bring the grains of salt in contact with the water, it is impossible not to have gritty butter where salt that is coarse or hard, or both, is used. All ground salts, and those made very dry by exposure to high temperature—that is, have the water of crystallization expelled—are objectionable on this account They dissolve too slowly, and the sharp angles of the particles made by grinding, cut the "grain" of the butter very rapidly.

It was a universal complaint among the judges of butter at the leading fairs held last season that it was over worked. On inquiry it was found that a good many butter makers were in the habit of using coarse grained salt under the mistaken notion, which had been instilled into their minds by salt agents, that fine salt which dissolved freely would incur waste—and, with their idea of "working in the salt, in an undissolved state, there was some force to this argument. The best butter exhibited at the Minnesota State Fair was that made by Mr. Leslie of Springfield, and which was awarded the Higgins prize silver pitcher, it was pronounced by the judges perfect in texture and scored 19 out a possible 20 points –the Chairman remarking "We must be careful how we mark *anything* perfect, " it was of course salted with Higgins "Eureka" Salt. The salting was done in the churn, by stirring the salt in without the least bit of working. The butter was taken from the churn in the granular form—Mr. Leslie said as fine as mustard seed—and put directly into the package, where it was for the first time pressed into a solid mass. All his butter was treated in this way. But, of course, without a fine, even-grained, freely-dissolving salt, this would be impossible.

With a large dairy or a factory, this may seem to some to involve a good deal of difficulty and labor. On the contrary, it saves both.

Some of the best creamery proprietors always salt their butter without working and pack it as soon as salted. It should be washed in brine and in water at 48 degrees, then take the butter out of the churn on to an inclined butter table, let it properly drain, sprinkle on the salt and rake it with a common hay rake. This will be found as convenient and effective a tool as can be got.

Begin on the edge and carefully haul a few granules towards you a little, then take a few more, and so on gently until the whole is gone over with. It is next raked crosswise, and the raking is continued until the salt is all dissolved. Of course, the moment the salt becomes brine, it settles all through the mass and covers every granule There is no other way of possibly getting the salt so evenly distributed through the butter. It is then ready for packing.

12

A WORD ABOUT SALT.

But, as already indicated, this method of salting and pack'ng butter will not do with all kinds of salt; yet it is the only method that leaves the texture perfect and the butter in its best condition for all purposes. The salt should have an even, natural grain, be perfectly and freely soluble, and free from all deleterious ingredients. Undoubtedly "salt is salt" the world over; but not all salt has the same impurities, nor in the same proportions, nor is all salt in the same condition. Hence there is wide difference in the different brands of salt—wider than most people suppose, when we come right down to the manufacture of the best possible article of butter.

The difference in the odor of different brands of salt indicates this contrast, for instance the clean pungent odor of chloride of sodium so apparent when you open a sack of freshly imported *Higgins* "Eureka" salt with the odor of other brands—especial'y some of our brands of domestic salt and the difference will be at once appa ent.

Dairy salt should be free from mechanical impurities—such as black specks, of which I have heard much complaint from users of ordinary salt, and pan scales, or flakes of sulphate of lime, which are found in some of the English and American brands. These get in from impurities settling on the bottom and sides of the kettles or pans, in boiling, and then scaleing off in thin flakes. They are claimed by some to be perfectly harmless. This might be if they remained in the scale form, when they would appear as hard lumps in dairy goods—a thing not to be desired, to say the least, but when they decompose, setting the sulphur and lime free, to remain so or to unite with other elements and form other compounds, they are far from harmless. If ground up with the salt, so they do not appear to the eye, as is the case where the grain is secured by grinding, they are no better. This does not get rid of them. On the contrary, it puts them into a more soluble form, so they sooner dissolve to injure the flavor of the product.

As to other specks and dirt in salt, they may come from careless manufacture or careless handling. The best salt can be spoiled by lazy handling—tumbling the sacks through the dust and dirt until they penetrated the material of the sack and mixed with the salt—most on the surface, of course, but rendering it impossible to get the salt out of the sacks free from fine dirt

Dealers are often guilty in this respect; salt is kept by them in places hardly fit for pig pens. It is in this way salt gets wet and then hardens and becomes inconvenient to use, if no other injury follows.

Again, salt kept in such a place, or in proximity to kerosene,

13

fish oils, codfish, herrings, or other bad smelling articles, or brought in contact with these in transportation, is often spoiled by absorbing these foul or disagreeable odors. Hence the complaint about *fishy* and other smells which we sometimes hear. Salt is about as sensitive to odors as any of the fats are. The tenacity with which it holds them is illustrated by the bottle of smelling salts which is often found in the pocket of a lady. In this case the salt is used to hold the pungent odor which the bottle gives out when uncorked. Salt will absorb and retain any other odors just as readily. Hence, too much pains cannot be taken to *keep salt in a clean, sweet place*, and to transport it in a cleanly manner. It should be handled and stored in at least as cleanly a manner as flour, which is no more liable to injury from improper handling and storing.

Sometimes we hear wooden packages recommended as the only fit ones for keeping salt. Undoubtedly, *if salt must be subjected to villianous usages*, wood is a great protection. But barrels are too expensive, and of little or no use when the salt is out. The dairyman does not want to pay twenty-five to fifty cents for a barrel that is of no real value to him when the salt is used. A sack has real value, and is of use in many ways. As by buying salt he gets the sacks at the cost of manufacture, it is an object to buy bags in this way, which may be of use in handling grain, or may be ripped open and used for toweling or other domestic purposes. Dairymen have decided preferences for strong linen sacks.

The preposterous claim has been set up that the use of a certain brand of salt not only improves the quality of the butter but adds to its weight. It is impossible for both claims to be true. In the first place, salt does not add to the quality of butter. If pure, the salt simply preserves whatever quality the butter has, and adds to it the sweet flavor of pure salt. If weight is added to the butter above that added by a freely-dissolving salt when the butter is sufficiently freed from water before salting, it is by the fraudulent retention of undissolved salt in the butter, thereby making it gritty and depreciating the market value of it two to five cents a pound. He is very short-sighted, therefore, who seeks to add to the weight of his butter by using hard, coarse-grained salt—for he depreciates its value ten times as much as he adds to its weight.

Naturally, the best salt is the highest-priced, each manufacturer knowing the value of his own product—the labor and care bestowed on its manufacture—and putting a market price on it accordingly. There are notable exceptions to this, however. The manufacturer who understands his business has an advantage over the one who lacks understanding. For illustration, Mr Thomas Higgin, of Liverpool, England, by his inventive genius and superior skill, not only *improved the quality of English dairy salt*, but materially reduced

14

the price of it to the American dairyman, who find the best foreign salt indispensable But the cost of even the highest-priced salt is but a trifle—less than a mill per pound to salt butter with it, and a correspondingly small cost per pound for cheese Three to five cents cover the entire cost of salting a 50 pound package of butter with the best salt in the market. Hence, it will poorly pay the dairyman to save on salt by using a cheap article, which must sooner or later depreciate the value of his butter, when by taking the higher priced he is sure of getting the best and of getting the best price for his goods when put upon the market "Penny wise and pound foolish" never made any man rich or happy. I have no doubt that millions of dollars are lost to the dairymen of the country every year by the use of poor salt

PACKING BUTTER.

Tubs for packing butter should be made of sweet wood—that is, wood that will impart no unpleasant flavor ; it should be thoroughly soaked to get out the woody flavor, and then saturated with brine Before packing sprinkle a little salt on the bottom of the tub—just enough to show—and rub the moist sides with salt, letting as much adhere as will, so as to prevent the wood from drawing the salt from the butter next to it as the water in the wood dries out A water-proof paper, odorless and flavorless, has recently been introduced, which is said to resist the action of salt, and to prevent all evapora tions when the tub is lined with it before filling Pieces are cut round and of any size to fit the ends of the tub ; and by the use of this paper, which is very cheap, it is claimed that a package may be made water-tight Pack in a way to expel the air and prevent its retention between the layers of butter

KEEPING BUTTER.

As soon as made, butter should be set in a cool, dry, sweet place, and kept at a temperature of about 50 degrees. Do not set the tubs on the ground, to absorb an earthy smell or flavor, nor per-mit any mold or decaying substance, or anything that gives an offen-sive odor, to be in the same apartment with the butter. Much good butter is spoiled by improper keeping and handling between the make-room and the consumption market

Why Higgin's "Eureka" Salt is Superior to others, and how it is made.

HIGGIN'S "EUREKA" SALT is prepared by a process peculiar to and patented by the manufacturer. It is manufactured from the brine of a natural brine-spring The brine is brought up from the earth, as a perfectly clear looking, sparkling liquid, which is allowed to rest in large reservoirs for some days before being drawn off for evaporation. It is then conveyed into pans, where it is subjected to a process which precipitates any insoluble matter held in suspension in it, and is afterwards drawn off into the evaporating pans, where it is heated up to the boiling p int. The salt precipitated in fine soft crystals is drawn from the pans at short intervals and is formed in molds into conical blocks, in which shape it is passed into ovens, and there it is thoroughly dried. When dry it is reduced from the conical blocks to its original separate crystals, and these are sorted into differe t sizes suitable for different uses, every particle of foreign impurity being removed during the process The machine separates the ci arse from the fine salt, and throws into the waste heap all pan scales etc. It is never handled during any part of the process of manufacture, but comes from the machines from different shutes according to size of grain, and falls at once into the sack, bag or packet in which it is exported or delivered to the consumer. Thus is produced salt chemically pure and in an eminently cleanly state.

It is a peculiar feature of this salt that the fineness of grain is not attained by grinding or crushing it either in the block or in the separate crystals, and the crystals delivered to consumers are the original, unbroken crystals precipitated during evaporation ; hence its fine flavor and its light, soft and free condition. The Higgin patented process is the only practical plan conceivable by which the pan scale and other impurities can be extracted whole and unbroken from salt.

"EUREKA" SALT is packed at the works in Cheshire, England, in four-i ushel and one-bushel pure linen sacks, which cannot be excelled for towelling or rubbing cloths. **For Household Purposes** it is put up in neat 14-lb. bags—16 in a good brown outer sack ; this is acknowledged to be the most desirable salt package ever offered.

HIGGIN'S "EUREKA" SALT can be used direct from the Bag without any further manipulation.

IT PAYS TO USE THE BEST SALT.

AN EXAMPLE.

There are 3,584 ounces in a sack of Higgin's Salt, costing, say, $3 00 If three-quarters of an ounce of salt to a pound of butter is used (or say 75 ounces to a hundred pounds of butter), the total cost of the salt used is a trifle over six cents per hundre l pounds of butter It may make a difference in the selling price of six cents per pound, or $6 00 per hundred pounds ; but suppose that it only makes a difference of one cent per pound, or one dollar per hundred, it is a pretty good reward for using the best salt.

ANOTHER EXAMPLE.

The total cost for the Higgin's Salt required to salt 100 pounds of cheese is only about three cents, and with common salt from one and a half to two cents. Suppose a cheese salted with the latter sold for a cent a pound less than that salted with the former, the producer would lose 50 cents in trying to save one cent.

Every sa't-maker claims that his brand is just as good, and that you cannot tell the difference between butter salted with Higgin's and other salt. Perhaps in some cases this may be true, but in such cases it is due to the skill of the butter-maker and the freshness of the butter more than anything else. Admitting, for the sake of argument, that "salt is salt," and that the difference in quality 's not readily apparent, if by using "everything of the best," the dairyman can ask and obtain a higher price for his product, whether of butter or cheese, is it not good judgment to use the best?

Why run any risk when the difference in cost between using Higgin's Salt and other brands is so very slight?

Is it not like the economy which would indu e a tailor to use bad thread in making up a good garment? Remember that the process by which Higgin's "Eureka" Salt is manufactured is the only one that the British Government ever honored with a patent, and that wh le it costs about one-third more to manufacture salt by Higgin's process than it does by any other process, the product is as much superior in quality to salt made by the old process as steel is to iron.

"Eureka" Salt is the purest, strongest and most uniform grained salt ever manufactured, and instances of the keeping qualities of butter and cheese cured with it have been remarkable.

The best of everything in dairy appliances and material is not too good to enable dairymen at the present time to compete in quality with other dairy countries in the markets of the world, and the wonderful increase in the sale of this "Eureka" Brand, and its use by the noted creameries that have won the premiums at the various butter and cheese exhibits, show that the best is appreciated.

Her Majesty, the Queen of England, uses "Eureka" Salt in her dairies. It is used in all the fancy dairies of England, Scotland, Ireland, Scandinavia and Holland. The most successful dairymen and creamerymen in the United States use it with sure results.

Other brands of salt a e not considered safe to use in the best English dairies.

CAUTION.

We caution purchasers against fraudulent imitations, as our style of package is being copied by other manufacturers, who put up common factory-filled salt "sifted."

NONE GENUINE UNLESS PROPERLY SEALED WITH THE COMPANY'S SEAL,   AND BRANDED WITH THE COMPANY'S BRAND AND REGISTERED TRADE MARK

Testimonials from Leading Authorities.

From the Queen's Dairy Farm

THE PRINCE CONSORT'S SHAW FARM,
WINDSOR

DEAR SIR,—We have used your Eureka Salt at the Royal Dairy for all purposes, and find it cleaner and purer than any we have ever seen. It mixes better with the the butter, and a much smaller quantity of this salt than of the ordinary kind is sufficient for flavoring and preserving. I can with confidence recommend it to all dairies

I am, dear sir, yours faithfully,
(Signed)   HENRY TAIT

From a Tenant of Lord Wilton

SPIN MOOR FARM, RADCLIFFE,
MANCHESTER,

MR THOS HIGGIN —Dear Sir   I have much pleasure in recommending the Eureka Salt   There is such a wonderful improvement in the quality and flavor of our butter that we shall use no other
Yours respectfully,
(Signed)   PETER STREET

I have used Higgin's Eureka Salt for the last year, and consider it superior to any other salt, and I have tried them all
LISBON, IA   B A RINGER

I have used Higgin's Eureka Salt, and consider it superior to any other brand for dairy use   H. C. CARTER
CONCORD, MINN

At this present time, out of two hundred or more customers, not one of them use any but Higgin's Salt   I should not handle Ashton Salt if I could get it for half price   W C WELLINGTON.
HARVARD, ILL

I have been selling Higgin's Eureka Salt for years to the best makers in our vicinity, and they give it the preference over all other brands
W. W. HOVER
MAZOMANIE, WIS

I have used the Higgin's Eureka Fine Salt for my butter, and am satisfied it is the best in use
(Signed)   PHILO WEBB
GREENE, N Y

I have introduced the Higgin Eureka Salt to all our leading dairymen, and it is meeting their wants better than any ever before introduced. Our grocers all find it is *the* salt they must keep to suit their customers, and we are having a better quality of butter in consequence
HOWARD MURPHY
BELFAST, ME

FROM HON. HIRAM SMITH.

*President N W Dairymen's Association.
(Mr Smith took the $450 Prize at the International Fair)*

I have used the Higgin Eureka Salt in both butter and cheese and am free to say I never used any better salt Its use for butter is preferable to any other I have used, because it is finer grain and is more readily dissolved—can be more evenly distributed through the butter, requiring less working, thereby better preserving the aroma, and it keeps the butter equally as well as any other salt
Respectfully,
HIRAM SMITH.
SHEBOYGAN FALLS, WIS

I believe the Higgin Eureka Salt to be superior to any other brand, and like it better than Ashton's. I have used it for years   A S BAREES,
Marple River Creamery
CHATEAUGAY, N. Y.

I have quit using Ashton's, and commenced using Higgin's Eureka   I consider it far ahead of any salt now on the market, being free from pan-scales, and sifted ready for use.   U GAULT
DWIGHT, ILL.

I have used the Higgin's Eureka Salt for my dairy, and am satisfied it is the best dairy salt in use   EVI STRATTON
SMITHVILLE, CHENANGO Co , N Y

Higgin's Eureka Salt has given us entire satisfaction   Everyone is pleased with it and considers it superior to Ashton's or any other brand
BOARDMAN BROS
NEVADA, IOWA
We have sold Higgin's Eureka Salt for a number of years   Our numerous customers speak of it in unmeasured praise For dairy purposes it has no equal, and for all uses where a strictly pure article is required it is superior to any other salt, such is the united judgment of our patrons and ourselves
FARNHAM, ALLEN & CO
COLUMBUS, WIS

I have used the Higgin Eureka Salt while foreman of C M. Sanborn's Creamery in this place, and in New York State, when acting as foreman of Hon E S Crapser'e Crystal Spring Creamery. I find the Higgin Salt superior to any other for the reason that it readily dissolves and leaves the butter with a more velvety texture than any salt ever used by me
FRIEND LEWIS
MAQUOKETA, IA.

18

FROM HON. HARRIS LEWIS.

President of the New York State Dairymen's Association.

In my system of making butter by the granular process, the size and form of the grain of Higgin's Eureka Salt is such that it is peculiarly adapted for salting it. A coarse grain salt like other imported salt requires at least twenty to twenty-four hours to assume the same condition that butter salted with Eureka does in six hours, rendering exposure to the atmosphere, whether good or bad, nearly four times as long as with Eureka. It is unnecessary for me to state that the sooner the salt is incorporated with the butter, and the butter packed, the more the natural and delicious flavor of the butter is retained.   HARRIS LEWIS

We are using Higgin's Eureka Salt, and consider it superior to Ashton's or any other salt as it is pure, and of better quality, and free from specks.
          JULIUS CHAPMAN
Kingston, Ill.   ———

Everyone writes that there is nothing equal to the Higgin's fine salt for butter and table use. Ashton's is not called for now. Now the cry is "Give us Higgin's Salt and we can give you choice butter."
          C H & W L BARRON

I am using Higgin's Eureka Salt, and am very much pleased with it. Consider it superior to Ashton or any other brand, and the sacks are fine linen.
          S. J DEARHOLT
Reedsburg, Wis.

I have used Eureka Salt for my butter the past season, and am satisfied that it is the best salt in use.
          CHAUNCEY SIMMONS
Greene, N Y

We are using Higgin's Eureka Salt in our dairy, and consider it better than any other brand, and recommend it to all dairymen   W H NEARPASS
Grandville, Mich.

I find the Higgin Eureka Salt a very superior article, and as near perfection as possible, according to the means I have of judging   S S SHATTUCK.
Norwich, N Y

The Higgin's salt gives good satisfaction   H A WILLIAMSON
Quincy, Ill.

We find Higgin's Eureka Salt preferable to any other brand. It dissolves more readily than Ashton, and is less liable to leave the butter streaked. All our best butter-makers use it.
          C H BEEMAN & CO
Minneapolis, Minn

I have tried the Ashton Salt and other varieties of salt in my dairy, but Higgin's Eureka Salt I use exclusively, and am confident it is the very best. I took first premium on my butter at the Broome Co Fair, the Oxford Fair, and at the Smithville Fair.   C E READ
Greene, Chenango Co., N. Y.

Every premium awarded by the Chautauqua Agricultural Society to-day was given to butter salted with Higgin's salt, and the committee, John Vanderburg and F A Picket, were pronounced Ashton men.   Yours,   A B CARTER
Jamestown N Y, Sept 2, 1886.

We regard Higgin's Eureka Salt as clean, pure salt, and consider dairies not using it as not advancing their best interests.   MRS. MARY L ROBBINS
Winthrop, Me

I consider Higgin's Eureka Salt the best in the market for dairy use. Have sold it for the last three years.
          R D McNAUGHTON,
Coopersville, Mich

I have sold Higgin's Eureka Salt for the last eight years. I find the demand for it largely increasing, and our dairymen who have once used it will use no other brand. I expect next season to double my sales on it.   C WALLACE
Oswego, N Y

We have been selling Higgin's Eureka Salt for years, and it is giving universal satisfaction.   H L SPENCER & CO
Oskaloosa, Ia

We consider Higgin's Salt the best salt we have ever sold free from pan-scales and specks. It gives entire satisfaction to the trade.   McKEE & SHELDON
Reedsburg, Wis

With my experience in the manufacture of butter and cheese, I consider the Higgin Eureka Salt superior to all other brands. In a fair trial it always comes out ahead, and I think will eventually supersede all others
Mexico, N Y   G A DAVIS

We consider Higgin's Eureka Salt superior to any salt we ever used.
          JEFFERSON COLVIN
Kingston Ill

From fifteen years' experience I know that Higgin's Eureka Salt is superior to all others   THOMAS SHEPHERD
Platteville, Wis

We have sold Higgin's Eureka Salt for years, and know it cannot be excelled
          E L & G D KENYON
Batavia, N Y

I have been in the dairy business for many years and consider Higgin's Eureka Salt superior to any other in the market, having taken the first premium on butter salted with it   W H GILL
Larned, Pawnee County Kansas

I use the Higgin Salt in my creamery and my foreman prefers it to the Ashton. It gives so good satisfaction that I shall order a car this week   W T SHAW
Anamosa Iowa

[Colonel Shaw is running several creameries, and is building more. Is one of the leading men of Iowa.]

19

We have used Eureka salt for several years with most satisfactory results We find it an improvement on Ashton's and other salt, it needs no sifting, is uniform in grain, free from impurities, thoroughly soluble and always reliable We use it for butter and cheese, and our products command the highest prices We find it pays to use the best salt

HUDSON, Ohio   S STRAIGHT & CO

[Messrs S Straight & Co are among the largest creamery and cheese-factory proprietors in Ohio]

This is to certify that I am furnishing several creameries (part of which I own) with the Higgin's Eureka Salt, and consider it superior to Ashton's or any other within our knowledge, for dairy or any other purpose that requires a No 1 salt

BRAIDWOOD, ILL   D RANKIN.

We have tested the Higgin Eureka Salt, and find it has no equal Send us seventy five sacks at once

DRIVER BROS & CO
DARLINGTON, WIS

I have used the Higgin's Eureka Salt for years and prefer it to any other in my dairy, it being free from specks and easier dissolved,   T BOST
EXCELSIOR, MINN

I have sold Higgin's Eureka Salt, and I consider it superior to any other brand of salt. It gives entire satisfaction to my customers   S MAYHRUN
GALENA, ILL,

I am using Higgin's Eureka Salt in my dairy, and like it better than any other salt I ever used   C. H CRANE
ROCHESTER, MINN

I am using Higgin's Eureka Salt, and consider it the best salt in the market Formerly used Ashton's, but do not consider that as good as the Higgin's
C W ACKERMAN
PALATINE, ILL

I have used only Higgin's Eureka Salt in my creamery for a number of years and want nothing better,
ELKHORN, WIS   D L FLACK

We have sold Higgin's Eureka only for the past six years It gives universal satisfaction Our dairymen will have no other.
EDSALL CHARDAVOYNE & CO
HAMBURG, N J

New York Farmers Club, Corning, N Y

Members of the Farmers' Club, having thoroughly tested the Higgin Eureka Salt, cannot speak in too high terms of its merits, and believe it to be the best salt now offered for preserving butter, the superiority of its manufacture placing it far in advance of Ashton, while it possesses all the good qualities claimed for Ashton

GEO P NIXON   M W ROBINS
ANDREW BOWNE   JAMES L PACKER
R MATTHEWSON   H D SMITH

We are using "Higgin's Eureka Salt" in the "Creston" Creamery We find it the finest article of its kind which we have ever been able to obtain, and no consideration would induce us to exchange it for any of the inferior brands which are upon the market   "With the Eureka Salt, to try is to buy," No sane man can possibly examine the salt and give it a trial, and be convinced that Mr. Higgin has not reached the pinnacle of excellence in the manufacture of his salt for dairy purposes It combines purity, cleanliness, and all the preservative qualities so essential to a fine salt in small, quickly dissolving translucent crystals
BUCKMAN & CO.
CRESTON, IA

I have used Higgin's Eureka Salt for the past year and consider it superior to Ashton's or any other brand   Everyone here is pleased with it
W. H HICKMAN, Sec'y,
Maple Grove Creamery.
SPRINGVILLE, IOWA

I am using Higgin's Eureka Salt in my dairy, and consider it splendid, and will use no other if I can get Higgin's
W M YOUNG
TOLEDO, CHASE COUNTY, KANSAS

I used Eureka and Ashton Salt in the butter exhibited at the Marengo Dairy Fair The tub salted with Higgin's Eureka took the first premium and with Ashton's, the second   F E MUNN
BELVIDERE, ILL

I have made butter and cheese *thirteen years*, and consider the Higgin Salt the very best for my purposes Butter salted with Higgin's Eureka Salt was sold for two cents per pound more than that which was made with any other
BENJ CHRISTIE.
SPRINGVILLE, Iowa

This is to certify that the salt used by me in the manufacture of the butter which drew the First Premium awarded at the Chautauqua County Fair N Y, for the best firkin made in September, and the best tub of butter made in September, was Higgin's Eureka Salt
L E FOSTER
JAMESTOWN, N Y

We sell the Higgin Salt, and our customers prefer it to any other as it is the very best.
H W & G W KERKER
DAVENPORT, IA

From a Minnesota Expert

This is to certify that the salt used in the manufacture of the butter which was awarded two first premiums at the World's Fair, at New Orleans, was salted with Higgin's Eureka Salt F. D HOLMES
OWATONNA, MINN

[A *Premium Taker*.— Mr. Frank D Holmes, Owatonna, Minn., at the late New Orleans Fair, took six out of twenty premiums offered on butter, and one-third the amount of money]

We have now made up our minds pretty decidedly on the subject of butter salt We have given careful trials to the Higgin, the Ashton, and to the leading American salts, and have given to the Higgin Salt the first place, and shall hereafter use it to the exclusion of all other kinds in our dairy. It is free from flakes and specks : it dissolves promptly and thoroughly, it is uniformly grained, and last and most important, it is wholly free from all bitter and acrid taste. If our Jersey cows will do their duty, and our farmers and dairymen theirs, the Higgin Salt will do all that any salt can do in the production of "gilt edged butter "

Sincerely yours,
RICHARD GOODMAN, Jr
Yokun Farm Lenox, Mass

[Mr Richard Goodman, Sr. is ex-President of the American Jersey Cattle Club, and Mr Goodman, Jr. the writer of the above, is the manager of the well-known Yokun Farm and the maker of the "gilt-edged butter" the product of that farm so well known in Massachusetts]

We are supplying a number of large creameries, and all regard the Higgin Eureka Salt as the best and most economical salt in use   It is also coming into general use among the farming community   H L SPENCER & CO
Oskaloosa Iowa

One cannot be too careful in working butter , it will have a salvie look and oily taste, no matter what salt they use, if worked too much   the more it is worked the more salt one must use and it destroys the flavor of the butter   Cleanliness is absolutely necessary from first to last

Yours,   S J GRIGG
Rutland, Vt

We have used the Higgin's Eureka Salt at our creamery since we commenced operations, and our butter has always sold at top prices. We are pleased to say that we consider this salt the best in the market, and having made as much as 2,000 pounds of butter per day, and never having a complaint as to its quality, we are led to the conclusion that the salt has done all that it is claimed it will do
W. B. CROMWELL,
Manager of Buena Vista Creamery
Storm Lake, Iowa

I am free to say that your salt gives better satisfaction than any other I have ever used   Being much finer and entirely free from hard substances, it dissolves much quicker , consequently butter does not need to stand so long between the first and second workings. Since using the Eureka salt we have not had one word of complaint about streaky butter. I shall use no other salt as long as I can get it We have perhaps the largest creamery in the State of Ohio, and use about 400 pounds of your salt per week
MALVERN CREAMERY CO ,
W S SHEPARD, Manager.
Malvern, Ohio, Sept 4th, 1886

From the Celebrated Oaklands Jersey Dairy
We have used various salts claimed as especially fine "Dairy Salt," but none have suited our requirements so thoroughly as Higgin's "Eureka Salt," and we consider it the most cleanly pure and uniform salt we ever used , when quality is sought we consider it the most economical, as according to our experience, no butter unless salted with your brand is acceptable to our customers
VELANCEY E FULLER,
Hamilton, Canada, March, 188

Four out of Five Experts Pronounce Higgin's Eureka Salt the Best.

A LITTLE EXPERIENCE MEETING

1, Will sweet cream 24 hours from the milk make as much, as good and as long keeping butter as sour cream or cream a little acid ? 2 Which is the better salt Ashton's or Higgin's to use for butter and which will keep butter the longer ? 3 Is the method of salting butter with brine desirable in large creameries? 4 Can the brine be used more than once to advantage ? 5 Can butter be made as salt with brine as by working in one ounce of salt to the pound ? 6 Do New England creameries use the brine method?—[Butter Maker

1 I think sour cream will make butter of longer keeping qualities Sweet cream will make nice butter to use up at once, but not so much of it 2 I don t think there is much difference I use Higgin's, an imported salt and like it very much 3 I use brine to wash the butter with and like the idea. I think it is a practice the creamery cannot do without 4 The brine can be used but once in a creamery ? No 6 I don't think many New England creameries use brine   These are all proper questions to discuss at the meeting of the proposed Association —[H L Cummings, Treasurer Co operative Cream ery Association, North Brookfield, Mass]

1 I think not. 2 I think Ashton salt is the stronger and will keep butter longer   3-6 I have never used brine, and know of no creameries that do —[J M Gladwin, Butter Maker, Canton Creamery, Canton Center, Ct

1 No 2 Higgin s 3 No 4, I think not 5-6 No , I know of no creameries that use the method exclusively —[H L Crandall Butter Maker, Farmington Creamery Farmington, Ct

1 Sweet cream, 24 hours from the milk, will not make as much, as good or as long-keeping butter as sour cream. 2, Higgin s salt is the best, and will keep butter the longest   3 Brine salting creameries may be desirable, but it takes four times as much salt as in working the salt in All customers do not want the same amount of salt 4 Brine can be used more than once by adding more salt. 5 Butter can be made nearly as salt with brine as by working in one ounce of salt to the pound [B C Bliss, Ashby Creamery Ashby, Mass

1 If it has been kept at about 60° it will 2 Higgin's Eureka salt is the most reliable and best in the market If butter is not made right it will change, no matter how good the salt is or how much is used. 3 Yes 4 When butter is made every day, the brine might be safely kept and used for a day or two It always gathers little buttermilk, which soon grows stale and would endanger the butter if used too long   5 Not without leaving in more brine than would be profitable to a purchaser If the brine is pressed out as closely as it should be it salts at the rate or about half an ounce to the pound 6, I have no personal knowledge of practices in New England creameries [Prof L B Arnold —in 'New England Homestead,' Sept 15, 1886)

21

From a Prominent Cheese Maker
I exhibited cheese salted with Onondaga, Ashton's and Higgin's salt. The cheese salted with Higgin's salt were placed first among U S cheese in the sweepstakes class. JOHN McADAM
ROME, N Y

This is to certify that I was awarded the two First Premiums at the Iowa State Fair of 1880, and two First Premiums again in 1881, with butter salted with the Eureka Salt I believe it to be superior to all others
C H, LYON, Dexter Creamery
DEXTER, DALLAS COUNTY, IOWA

From the Winner of the Highest Award on Dairy Butter at the New Orleans Exposition
I won the "Higgin Cup" two years ago at our county fair, and have taken the first premium on butter three years in succession at the same place, and give due credit to the salt Our prize butter at New Orleans was salted with Higgin's Eureka salt Very respectfully,
J G FLACK,
ELKHORN, Wis , April 13, 1885

Having used Ashton's Salt formerly, I was induced to try the Higgin's Eureka, and the Judges of the N B C and I Association pronounced the butter salted with the Eureka, the best
A M ROWE, Vinton Creamery
VINTON, IOWA

From a Texas Authority
This is to certify that I have for years used the Higgin Eureka Salt only, and that at thirty exhibitions I have taken twenty-eight first premiums at the fairs of Texas, and that I am not willing to exchange it for any other salt,
D COULSON
Alderney Creamery
SAN ANTONIO, Texas

Extract from Letter
I like it ever so much It is so clean and nice, and is real good It is a first-class salt MRS J W SANBORN
Wife of Prof Sanborn, Missouri Agricultural College
COLUMBIA, Mo , June 24, 1886

We want only Higgin's Eureka Salt, and will use no other salt for butter if we can get that
MAPLE GROVE CREAMERY
SPRINGVILLE, Ia

I have used the Ashton Salt for many years in my dairy, considering it the best salt obtainable The only fault I found with it was the little black specks which had to be sifted out before using it, and frequently we had to break it up with the rolling-pin on account of its coarseness Since using Higgin's Eureka Salt I have no trouble I always find it of uniform grain, perfectly free from impurities It dissolves readily and gives me full satisfaction I recommend it to other dairymen as a far superior article
CORTLAND, N Y P H SEARS

Your salt has been used in our dairy for two seasons, and has proved entirely satisfactory Respectfully,
ONEIDA COMMUNITY (Limited)
By WM A HINDS,
COMMUNITY, N Y July 15, 1886

We formerly used the Ashton, but changed a year ago to Higgin's Eureka, and like it the best. It is free from dirt, pan-scales, etc, ' and gives a finer aroma to our butter.
CLARK & BEARD BROTHERS
ELWOOD, IOWA

Kalamazoo Co. (Mich) Agricultural Society
The Executive Committee of the Kalamazoo County (Mich) Agricultural Society have thoroughly examined the Higgin's Eureka Salt, at our last County Fair In our judgment it is the best salt now in use for preserving butter, the superiority of its manufacture placing it in advance of any other salt
W H COBB, President
FRANK LITTLE, Secretary
W. H. McCOURT, Treasurer

Having used many kinds of salt for forty years in the butter business, I find none equal to the Higgin Eureka Salt I have used and sold it for five years, and would not use any other I sell it to dairymen exclusively, all like it to a man
RENNSELAER RUSSELL
WATERLOO, IA.

Prof Shelton, of our college, turned over to me a sack of Eureka salt for use in the college dairy I found it the cleanest salt we have ever had, and it was in all respects very satisfactory to use, it seemed perfectly pure, and was finer than most of the dairy salt I have used before
N S, KEDZIE
Dept Household Economy,
Kansas Agricultural College,

Having handled your Eureka Salt for years, and included among our customers the butter shippers of this country, we report only the one verdict they all give, that it is the best in use
COOPER, SPEAR & CO
MARSHALLTOWN, IA

New York Agricultural Experiment Station
(Extract from Letter)
The Higgin's Eureka Salt has given us most excellent satisfaction
DR E L STURTEVANT,
Director N Y. Agricultural Experimental Station, GENEVA, N Y , June 24, 1886

Higgin's Eureka Salt is ahead of any salt we have ever tried, for the reason that it is free from lumps and specks and has no bad flavor, and we think the butter when salted with it keeps better than with any other salt we have us d We think it of great value to the dairying interest C MILLER & SON.
POMFRET, Vt , April 8, 1885

22

This is to certify that at the annual fair of the Walworth County Agricultural Society, held at Elkhorn, September 20 to 24, I was awarded the first of the special premiums, of $25, offered by Thomas Higgin, of Liverpool, England, for the best package of butter salted with Higgin's Eureka Salt, also that I was awarded the first premium offered by the Agricultural Society for the best package of creamery butter I use nothing but Eureka Salt, considering it the purest, best grained, and easiest handled of any salt used
ELKHORN, WIS   G A LYTLE

The Almoral Creamery use with entire satisfaction the Higgin Eureka Salt, and commend it for its purity and superior qualities over the Ashton or any other salt heretofore used   L E STEVEN
ALMORAL, DELAWARE CO , IOWA

Michigan Agricultural College   Farm Department
(Extract from Letter)
Higgin's Eureka Salt is pronounced first class   SAM'L JOHNSON
                    Prof of Agriculture
July 15, 1883

Houghton Farm, Mountainville Orange Co
(Extract from Letter)
We keep Higgin's Eureka always in store, and use nothing else in salting our butter   HENRY E ALVORD,
                    Prof Experimental Station
N Y, Dec 1, 1885

Higgin's Eureka Salt is the kind for Iowa dairymen   ASA C BOWEN
SAND SPRING, IOWA

We consider Higgin's Salt the purest and best salt, and use it in our creamery
                    S & F P ROWE,
                    Glenwood Creamery
WEST HAMPTON, IOWA

University of Nebraska   Industrial College Farm
(Extract from Letter)
Eureka Salt seems to be of very excellent quality   H H WING,
Instructor in Agriculture and Farm Supt
LINCOLN, Neb , June 25, 1886

I have used your salt for the past three years in the manufacture of Jersey butter, and am pleased to say that I consider it superior to any salt I have ever used
                    C P MATTOCKS
PORTLAND, Me , Jan 19, 1885

I am pleased with Higgin's Eureka Salt and consider it superior to any other It dissolves more readily in the butter It stands at the head   R P BROWN
GRAND JUNCTION, IOWA

This is to certify that the salt used in the manufacture of the butter which was awarded the first premium at the annual meeting of the Minnesota State Dairymen's Association, held at St. Paul, 1880, for the Best Dairy Butter, was Higgin s Eureka Salt   WILLIAM FOWLER,
          Pres Minn Dairyman's Association.
NEWPORT, MINN.

We desire to state that at the Caledonia County Fair, held at this place all three of the prizes offered for June butter were awarded to butter salted with Higgin's EUREKA Also the first and third prizes for September butter, leaving only one second prize for butter salted with other kinds of salt The competition was very great, and the facts were fully established that this salt would keep butter until the fall better than any other kind, and that the only way to get the full value of summer butter is to use such salt as is sure to preserve it until the fall without changing flavor
Respectfully,   E T & H K IDE
ST JOHNSBURY, VT

Send me another car load of Higgin's Eureka Salt. It is used by nearly all the creameries and best dairymen about here, and gives entire satisfaction Could not do without it   JAMES HERSEY
EARLVILLE, IA

University of Wisconsin   Agricultural Experiment Station
Your salt is in every way satisfactory, and we shall continue to use this brand as long as it keeps to its present standard
                    W A HENRY,
                    Professor of Agriculture.
MADISON, Wis , June 27, 1885

Extract from Letter
Eureka salt has been used in our dairy, and in my judgment it is a first-class salt
                    L P ROBERTS
          Prof Agricultural Department,
          Cornell University,
ITHACA, N Y , June 25, 1886

From the Winner of the Highest Award on Butter over Southern States at the New Orleans Exposition
I used Higgin's Eureka dairy salt in the butter that took first premium over Southern States at the New Orleans Exhibition I have never used any other salt in my dairy Very truly yours,
                    JNO H ODINEAL,
JACKSON, Miss , April 6, 1885

I have used Higgin's Eureka Salt and consider it superior to Ashton's, or any other dairy salt in use It is more easily worked into the butter, and in every instance it has given perfect satisfaction
                    E E PAGE
MARSHALLTOWN IOWA

IS THIS NOT A GOOD REASON ?

When the difference in the cost of using Higgin's Eureka Salt and the cheapest American salt is only about one-thirteenth of a cent a pound on butter and one-sixteenth of a cent a pound on cheese, and it might make fifty times this difference in the value of the product, one would think that butter and cheese makers would not hesitate long in deciding what salt they would use

23

CPSIA information can be obtained
at www.ICGtesting.com
Printed in the USA
LVHW081529311018
595483LV00015B/265/P

9 781298 804754